Engaging the Parking Lot Parent

A CATECHIST'S GUIDE TO FOSTERING PARENT PARTICIPATION

SR. PATRICIA M. MCCORMACK, IHM, ED.D.

TWENTY-THIRD PUBLICATIONS

twentythirdpublications.com

TWENTY-THIRD PUBLICATIONS
One Montauk Avenue, Suite 200
New London, CT 06320
(860) 437-3012 or (800) 321-0411
www.twentythirdpublications.com

Cover Illustration: ©iStockphoto.com/kchungtw

ISBN: 978-1-62785-253-1
Library of Congress Control Number: 2016960018
Printed in the U.S.A.

A Division of Bayard, Inc.

CONTENTS

Introduction

I t was time for breaking open the word with the little children. Young minds eagerly listened to the account of Jesus calling the twelve apostles and sending them, two by two, to preach the Good News. The six-year-olds were spellbound. After the reading they shared how they could each be an apostle for Jesus throughout the following week. Their catechist, Miss Emma, told the class about a particular way they could be apostles that very day. She distributed a flyer advertising a "Dad's Retreat." She encouraged the children to be apostles to their fathers by placing the flyer in their hands. As an extra incentive, Miss Emma offered a beautiful statue of Jesus as a prize to the first student who brought back the invitation signed and dated by his or her father.

While the children were engaged in their final activity, little Keira burst into the room with a signed flyer in hand. She happily announced, "I won! I won! I am the first apostle! My dad signed the paper!"

Miss Emma was shocked that Keira had left the session without her knowledge. She was also stunned that Keira interrupted the community at Mass to find her father. And she felt threatened by the mutiny in the room as other students called out, "No fair! No fair!" Miss Emma quieted the class and then asked Keira how she managed to be the first apostle. "Did you go into church and interrupt Mass?" "Oh, no!" replied Keira. "It's my dad's turn to drive to church, so he's in the parking lot waiting for me."

Dad was in the parking lot rather than at Mass. Such a scene is not uncommon. A sizable number of parents spend an hour in their cars while their children are attending Mass or a faith-formation class. One catechetical leader describes them as the "taxi community."

This scenario raises a critical question among pastors, catechetical leaders, and catechists: How do we draw parents into the parish and out of whatever "parking lot" keeps them disengaged and non-participative?

In my role as a national formation-education consultant and public speaker, I deliver presentations throughout the United States to parents, teachers, catechists, catechetical leaders, and school administrators. These groups often bemoan the lack of parent participation in the formation of their offspring. In many instances catechists report how students are unprepared for class, parents are disengaged from the process of faith formation, and religious/spiritual development of children seems limited to the time spent in a religion class. They report poor church attendance among the adults.

The problem runs deeper than not just showing up. In 1990 Saint John Paul II expressed concern that "entire groups of the baptized have lost a living sense of the faith, or even no longer consider themselves members of the Church, and live a life far removed from Christ and his Gospel. In this case what is needed is a 'new evangelization' or a 'reevangelization'" (*Mission of the Redeemer*, 33).

What can be done to encourage, support, and affirm parents so that they feel invited and inspired to engage in their own faith development as well as that of their children? In this book I offer ideas for reaching out to those who are minimally, marginally, or insufficiently involved in the faith formation of their children and who are themselves in need of evangelization. Thus the goal of this book is to lead parents from the "parking lot" of non-involvement to participation in the faith formation of their children and ultimately to a personal encounter with Jesus.

Chapter 1

A VIEW FROM THE PARKING LOT

How do parents view their role when it comes to the faith formation of their children? Some feel inadequate as the spiritual leader in the family. Others note the need for someone other than themselves to form faith within their children. Liz Lockhart, Parent and Youth Faith Formation Director at St. Joseph Parish, Marion, Iowa, offers a keen insight into this dilemma:

> Parents are willing to abdicate our role as teachers of our children in a variety of areas—sports, academic tutoring, and even hiring people to drive our children to activities when we are too busy to do so. We have no hesitance when it comes to expecting others to teach our children the Catholic faith, especially if we feel inadequate in our attempts to do so. The danger is forgetting that anything that isn't modeled in the home probably

won't take root in our children's lives over the long
haul. Furthermore, those "experts" may not know
much more than we do. They just are more willing
to spend the time to learn it and pass it along.

I hear similar sentiments during my own interactions with
parents. When discussing the difference between their role
as parents and that of the catechist, one mother noted that
the catechist has the teacher edition of the book. Another
parent piggybacked on that remark by saying, "Catechists
are trained; we are not." A dad pointed out that catechists are
deeply involved in the parish and have knowledge of church
teachings that he lacks. Their responses affirm the role of the
catechist and reflect a trust in what he or she is doing for
their children.

REASONS FOR DISENGAGEMENT
In order to overcome the obstacles to engagement by some
parents, it's helpful to name them first. Then we can more
effectively develop strategies that invite involvement and
participation. Here are three common obstacles I have come
across in the course of my work with parents.

1. Inadequate knowledge of their faith and a need for evangelization

The need for evangelization or reevangelization stems, in
large part, from a lack of knowledge or understanding of
Catholic teachings and practices. Parent explanations vary for
their surface knowledge of the Catholic faith but here are
some of the perceptions I have come across:

- Post-Vatican II changes in liturgical worship as well as changes in some church disciplines have caused some 1970s parents (current-day grandparents) to think, "What I was taught might be different today." And so they hesitate in passing on church teaching. It is not at all unusual for a parent or grandparent to wonder aloud, "Is it still true that…?" As a result, some of these 1970s parents feel confused and have lost confidence in their ability to instruct their children and grandchildren in the practices of the faith. They conclude that it is better to say nothing rather than chance being incorrect. As a consequence, they feel illiterate in terms of faith formation and have ceased to be a source of Catholic formation for their children. Their offspring (current-day parents) grew in a spiritual vacuum. When they became parents themselves they felt inadequate to assume the role of "First Heralds of the Gospel." The cycle continued to the present generation of parents.

- The formal formation of today's parents was brief and spotty. Publisher programs are skillfully designed to condense a grade curriculum into manageable pieces. Nevertheless, "mastery" of each lesson must rely upon follow-up at home. This creates "hit and miss" catechesis. In addition, many students stopped attending religious education classes in middle school after they received the sacraments of Eucharist, penance, and confirmation.

- As a consequence of the drop in regular participation in Sunday Mass and parish devotions, there is a growing lack of familiarity with the teachings and rituals of the

Catholic faith. Unless parents were vitally involved in a well-rounded parish youth group, their high-school education in the Catholic faith was limited to the Sunday homily (if the person attended Mass) and, perhaps, to instruction contained in a church bulletin or brochure.

- The *General Directory for Catechesis* cites the importance of a broad approach to the catechetical ministry. The religious education program of their youth (1970s–1980s), however, often put so much emphasis on social justice awareness that it failed to integrate all six tasks of catechesis as defined by the GDC: knowledge of the faith, liturgical education, moral formation, learning to pray, education for community life, and missionary initiation (GDC 84).

- Time constraints in the one-hour weekly sessions restrict the religious curriculum to "bare bones." Limited instruction time interferes with learning the *meaning* behind the commandments, the sacraments, prayer, customs, and rituals. Without meaning and appreciation, church practices become mere external observances rather than rich experiences of relationship with God. Consequently, these parents often developed a mentality of burden rather than a sense of privilege, love, and relationship.

- At the conclusion of the Second Vatican Council, distinctions between "conservative" and "liberal" influenced programs of religious education. Tensions arose that led some religious educators to mistakenly link the concept of "conservative" with the term "traditional." The reactionary outcome was to eliminate from the curriculum some perennial classic values and rituals that transcend time and trends—observances that identify us as Catholic, such as Eucharistic devotions (Benediction, Holy Hour/ Adoration, visits to the Blessed Sacrament), Marian devotions (the Rosary, novenas, May processions), and pious practices like saying aspirations, praying the noonday Angelus, walking the Stations of the Cross, or emphasizing the lives of saints. Such traditional marks of Catholic culture were eliminated without substitution, thus leaving a void. Grandparents and parents of pre-Vatican II days wondered what was left to pass on to their children.

- The Bible was central to the proceedings of Vatican Council II, which made sacred Scripture fundamental to prayer and religious education. Gathering for a "Bible service," "breaking open the word of God," "praying with Scripture," and designing Scripture-focused programs of religious education became the new norm. What a grace! Spiritual growth has happened and continues to occur because of personal prayer with the gospels. But at the same time, many parents felt like novices—unfamiliar with Scripture—because private reading of the Bible was not the experience of pre-Vatican II Catholics. Consequently, some parents did not know how to pray with Scripture, and they felt inadequate to teach their children the word of God.

- Large numbers of parents received no guidance to transition them from the faith-knowledge/formation of their childhood to an adult, personally responsive relationship with God. Any adult human relationship that is "stuck" in an adolescent dynamic is doomed to stagnate. If the perceptions, beliefs, dialogues, and memories of a teenage couple dominate their relationship at age thirty, that adult relationship is doomed to failure. This reasoning also applies to relationship with Jesus. Parents whose God-relationship is limited to their experiences in adolescence are in need of evangelization.

- Some catechists and Catholic school teachers received inadequate religious education in their own childhood. Unless they pursued a theology background in college or participated in ongoing formation-education programs, they had content and experiential gaps similar to their parent contemporaries. Additionally, many catechists were generous, zealous volunteers but lacked formal education in classroom management or teaching techniques. The combination of these conditions limited the effectiveness of their parish faith-formation programs. In some instances, this situation continues to persist today.

For various reasons, some people viewed themselves as unacceptable and unloved by the church; therefore, they severed allegiance to it and developed a disinterest in its affairs. "Some people simply have never had an encounter with Christ. Some have been baptized but have never personally appropriated the gift of faith. Some have been catechized but have left the faith community out of indifference, societal factors, hurt, scandal, etc." (*The Catechetical Leader in the Third Millennium*, a Statement of the Catholic Bishops of New York State, 2011, 8). Some in mixed marriages yielded their faith practices to the preference of their spouse. Some—because of divorce and remarriage without an annulment, or other situations—were excluded from the sacramental life of the church. Some, from a very young age, heard a church representative say that their lifestyles excluded them from participation. And others perceived that they endured unnecessary stress and hassle related to making plans for a wedding or a baptism or a funeral. They walked away and never looked back.

2. Cultural Shifts and Challenges

Parents lack the supportive public environment that Catholics once experienced. The late Bishop Ken Untener summarized the transition from Christian culture to a secularized, perhaps even pagan, culture:

> Times have changed. Sunday mornings are filled
> with entertaining TV shows, swim meets, league
> games, and travel demands. Holy Days have given
> way to commercialized holidays. It is not that
> people have become irreligious. No. The rhythm of
> life has. The social rhythm of life is no longer
> automatically tuned in to the practice of
> Christianity...If I am going to practice the Christian
> tradition of daily prayer (and other spiritual
> practices), I'm going to have to be
> "countercultural"—a bit out of step.
> **(UNTENER, LITTLE WHITE BOOK, 2003, EPILOGUE)**

Factor in the additional cultural challenges parents face today, such as the rise of secularism, the glorification of affluence, and pervasive media influences, and the shrinking of a Catholic culture becomes all the more apparent.

3. Busy Schedules and Commitments

Some parents are overwhelmed by the frantic pace of society and by the expectations of others as well as themselves. Additional challenges include arranging for multiple extracurricular school activities and student social events, caring for aging parents, working second jobs, providing for childcare, or seeking professional help for children with social, emotional, or specialized learning needs.

The view from the parking lot—that is, from the parents' perspective—offers some insights into the various reasons for minimal involvement in their child's religious formation. In the next chapter, we will explore ideas and strategies for easing some of these concerns by meeting needs and inviting parents into participation. This offers more than just a way to move parents out of the parking lot. It also invites them into fuller engagement with their own faith.

FOR REFLECTION AND DISCUSSION

1. *What favorite Scripture verses have you committed to memory? How experienced are you in praying with Scripture? Share an instance.*

---

2. *Because some parents lack knowledge of Catholic teaching, rituals, and practices, they feel unequipped to provide the religious formation of their children. As a faculty or parish team how can you combat these obstacles?*

---

3. *Perennial classic values and rituals transcend time and trends. What kinds of observances identify your religious education program as "Catholic"? What does your program do well? What could your program do better?*

---

4. *The GDC identified six tasks of catechesis: knowledge of the faith, liturgical education, moral formation, learning to pray, education for community life, and missionary initiation. As a faculty or parish team, prioritize the tasks and develop a plan to foster growth.*

Chapter 2

BACKDOOR EVANGELIZATION

The New Evangelization involves outreach to those who were baptized, confirmed, and received First Eucharist but have had no personal experience of Jesus. Cardinal Walter Kasper expressed the situation this way: "Many today are baptized, but not evangelized. Formulated paradoxically: they are baptized catechumens or even baptized pagans" (Kasper, *The Gospel of the Family*, 2014, p. 4). In other words, their hearts were never set ablaze.

Evangelization speaks first to the heart before trying to reach the head. Saint Pope John Paul II said, "We shall not be saved by a formula but by a Person, and the assurance which he gives us: I am with you!" (*Novo Millennio Ineunte* [apostolic letter on the close of the Jubiliee Year (2000], 39). The New Evangelization is an opportunity for catechists to be catalysts of grace for parents and to lead them to an experience of personal relationship with Jesus. This requires sensitivity to parents who feel inadequate when it comes to passing the faith on to their children. Catechists need to evangelize without antagonizing, offending, embarrassing, speaking down, adding stress, or implying guilt. In short, the goal is to energize rather than add to parent burdens.

I suggest that an effective way to begin the process of evangelizing parents is through the back door. That is, provide parents with opportunities for indirect learning by engaging them in interactions with their child that bring both parent and child into a deeper relationship with Jesus. By focusing on the child, a parent is able to relax and be non-defensive and non-threatened. Meanwhile, he or she learns faith content and may absorb the grace of encountering Jesus. "Backdoor" evangelizing builds up a parent's confidence level. At the same time, parents pick up tips from catechists and other parents who model how to communicate faith within the family. Take the example of Kathy Batz, a former catechetical leader, who used the catechumenal process to evangelize parents:

> I initiated the RCIC (Rite of Christian Initiation for Children). My requirement was that at least one parent accompany the child/ren to each session. Students from third grade through high school were together at the same time. I was able to teach such a wide age range because the parents were there. A parent could help the third grader understand and could discuss with the teen. These parents were mostly unchurched, which is why their children weren't baptized. I spent lots of time after class talking with parents and answering their questions. They were dealing with divorce,

abandonment, being away from the church for
many years…Because parents felt free and safe
enough, they would share with me all sorts of
stories of the issues with which they struggled.
Some returned to active participation as a result of
the RCIA experience.

Nonengaged parents who feel inadequate in matters of faith
formation need the help of catechists who will expose them
to family spirituality and provide glimpses into doctrine
and catechism content. Catechists as backdoor evangelizers
introduce parents to rituals, customs, and faith traditions
that touch the heart and nourish a sense of spirituality in
family life. By becoming familiar with routines, practices,
physical reminders, and expressions of faith that integrate
awareness of God into the home, parents grow more confi-
dent about passing on the traditions of the Catholic faith.
Examples of family practices are limited only by human creativity, energy level, and time availability.

Here are ten family practices catechists can suggest to parents as a way to raise awareness of God's presence in their
family.

- Establish a **Prayer Center**. Use a window sill, a tiered
  corner shelving unit, a table, the top of a filing cabinet—
  someplace that family members pass daily. Display the
  Bible, a rosary, prayer tools, etc.

- Provide a **Prayer Dish**, that is, a lidded container to hold
  prayer intentions. At mealtime or bedtime, pray, "for the
  needs that are included in our prayer dish." Empty the
  container during Advent, and use strips of the paper

petitions as straw for the Christmas crib; or burn them during Lent and use the ashes as fertilizer in the garden.

- Maintain a **Liturgical Centerpiece on the dinner table.** Use the liturgical color of the season with a thought-a-day calendar or a miniature easel to hold a focus picture or quotation, and/or place symbols related to feasts that occur during Ordinary Time, i.e., picture of the Sacred Heart, birthday candle for Mary (Sept. 8), Crown of Christ the King (End of November), etc.

- Hang a **Family Motto** banner above the entrance to the common room, i.e., "Do whatever he tells you." "Love one another." "God is with us now." "How have you shown love for the family today?" "As for me and my household, we will serve the Lord" (Joshua 24:15).

- Choose a **Family Mantra.** For instance,

  Leader: God is good all the time!
  Response: And all the time, God is good!

Or *Leader:* As for me and my family…
  Response: We will serve the Lord.

- Punctuate **Mealtime** with prayer before and after meals.

- Customize **Ritual Blessings** for
  (1) wakeup, for example:

    Parent: "Good morning, [name].
            You are a gift from God."
    Response: "And everything God makes is good";

(2) *bedtime*, for example:
    Parent: "Good night, [name], and God bless you.
            May he watch over you and keep you
            and make you grow up to be a good
            and healthy girl/boy;

(3) for *leaving the house*, for example,
    Parent: "May your Guardian Angel protect
            you and return you safely to me."

- Employ a **Conversation Starter** when it is necessary to have a critical conversation with a child. For instance, "May the Word of God be +in our minds, +on our lips, +and in our hearts throughout our conversation."

- Choose a feast day to be an **Annual Marker Day** for your family. For instance, celebrate Christ the King Sunday, the last Sunday in Ordinary Time. Include family Mass, plan a special meal or food reserved for this annual event, and reconsecrate your family to the service of Jesus, the Servant King by doing a family project like serving at a soup kitchen, nursing home, or women's shelter on this day.

- Designate one meal a week for **God Table Talk**. Ask a question like, "What is one way that you recognized or experienced God today or this week?" or "What is one way that you needed God's help today or this week?"

Some catechists report positive backdoor results merely from engaging parents to take turns serving as teacher aides for a class session. During the class these parent aides hear the lesson, experience the style of delivery, observe techniques for engaging children, and benefit from the catechist's passion and spirituality.

In some cases it might be sufficient to include one "backdoor thought" as a blurb in a parish newsletter or printed communication from the office. For example, in Advent: "Jesus is the reason for the season." Or, in Ordinary Time: "God loves you just the way you are, but he refuses to leave you that way. He wants you to be just like Jesus" (Max Lucado). Many a time a one-liner has caught my attention and led to prayerful connection. Most recently my heart was tutored by this quotation: "Do not put a period where God has placed a comma!"

PLAN GROUP EVENTS FOR BACKDOOR EVANGELIZATION

Fun and faith can go together! While focusing on the fun aspect of a church event, it is likely that faith will be kindled within some adult hearts. For instance, years ago I enjoyed an elementary-school production of a Christmas play called *Angels Aware* (Creative Ministry Solutions). The storyline was delightful, the dialogue was instructive, and the songs were lively. To this day certain lines from the production and lyrics from its songs pop up at moments when I need their wisdom.

Design events to be social in nature—interactive and conversational. Perhaps schedule the events to be intergenerational. Here is a model of a two-hour "People of Faith" event used by Our Lady of Mount Carmel Church in Newport News, VA.

> *Advertisement invited children and "parents, grandparents, godparents, and all who hand on the faith" to participate in a Mini-Scripture Camp. The event focused on how our baptismal promise to be priest, prophet, and king translates into daily family life. (Background was provided by **www. ParentTeacherSupport.org**....Newsletters/Family Faith/A Guide to Catholic Parenting.)*
>
> *The day opened with song, procession, and prayer. Children were dismissed to engage in worksheets and craft activities related to baptism while parents participated in the catechesis of baptism. Families reassembled to participate in a concluding activity.*
>
> *Parent catechesis included a brief PowerPoint overview. Chart papers were posted around the room with the headings of priest, prophet, and king. On sticky notes adults wrote down practical ways to function in those roles, and they posted the ideas on the appropriate charts.*
>
> *Families reassembled to create a family scriptural rosary. The leader introduced the concept of creating a "who-clause Hail Mary." An assigned gospel story was presented in both English and Spanish. Families read the gospel and from it created a "who clause" to complete the word "Jesus" in the Hail Mary. For instance, "Hail Mary full of grace the Lord is with you. Blessed are you among women and blessed is the fruit of your womb, Jesus, who desires us to help others without being asked, as he did for the Widow of Nain" (Lk 7:11–17).*

In round-robin fashion, families spoke aloud their "who clause" Hail Mary. The variety of responses affirmed the power of the Holy Spirit working through family experiences. On paper plates, children drew what the gospel meant to them, or they wrote the family "who clause." The plates were hung in groups of ten to form decades of the rosary.

The event concluded with a prayer of consecration to the Holy Family.

Create activities that are non-threatening. Plan for information to be self-correcting so that no parent is embarrassed by performance. Coordinate events with other catechists; use teamwork to develop themes, details, and materials. Share what works with other parishes; swap ideas parish-to-parish. Build up a repertoire of "Family Faith 'n' Fun Events" so that you can schedule an event with minimal exertion. Engage parent volunteers to "work" the events. In time, build up a committee who will sponsor such events.

PUMP PRIMERS FOR BACKDOOR EVANGELIZATION
When well water lies dormant, pumping it requires exterior action to force air out of the intake pipe and to generate suction that pulls water up and out of the well. That action is called priming the pump. The image applies to the following suggestions, since they are merely starter ideas to stir your own creative juices and to evoke additional practices. Adapt the following pump primers to your setting, and design others of your own.

*1. Set aside one class session each semester for parents to ac-
company their children and engage in fun by playing games.*
Tech-savvy folks can really add spice to the night! Network
with other teachers so that each teacher prepares only one
topic and the families move from classroom to classroom or
table to table. Simple activities include bingo, tic-tac-toe,
concentration, relay games, fill-in-the-blanks, and word
matching tests, all involving vocabulary and definitions. For
example:

- Catechetical program materials for religious formation
  classes as well as publisher Internet sites include work-
  sheets of "Catholic Trivia" and/or end-of-unit summary
  fact sheets.

- Focus on Catholic Culture. Use topics like
  Commandments, Sacraments, Saints, Rituals/Practices
  (like Stations of the Cross, the Rosary, formula for
  confession), details of Catholic disciplines (like holy days
  of obligation, fast, abstinence) and common prayers.

- Focus on characters from the Hebrew Scriptures,
  Christian Scriptures, and church history.

- Familiarize families with the format of the Bible. Search
  citations to complete a quotation; match a vocabulary
  word/personal name with a description; or assign a
  gospel story to each family. Appoint a time for the
  family to act out the story for others in the room.
  Instruct the family to suggest a "life lesson" that all
  members might apply in the week that follows.

- Deliver messages that touch the heart. For instance, use an inspirational e-mail "forward" for parent-child discussion, a child-oriented movie or cartoon with questions that touch the heart, or simple stories like those found in *Chicken Soup for the Soul*.

- Design a Computer Lab Passport Project. A passport collects stamps that validate international travels. Create a passport-style book or a handout sheet that indicates various website activities or YouTube clips for parent and child to view and discuss. Integrate the free material that Catholic publishers like RCL, Liguori, and Sadlier make available.

- Design a Mary Marathon event. Orchestrate breakout sessions/activities to focus on Mary—for example: audiovisual presentations of various apparitions (like Fatima, Lourdes, Guadalupe, Miraculous Medal/St. Catherine Labouré); the Rosary (the meaning of its prayers and how to make a rosary); titles in the Litany of the Blessed Virgin Mary; Marian art and symbolism; creating a family character rosary; multicultural representations of Mary; and major Marian feast days.

2. Orchestrate *"make and take" sessions for (1) pre-Advent, (2) pre-Lent, and (3) Ordinary Time.* Demonstrate ways to "honor" the season in the home. Background information is available at *www.ParentTeacherSupport.org*. (At this site, go to Newsletters/Family Faith/Creating a Spiritual Culture.) Engage program parents to bring to the session a different symbol/idea along with printed instructions and materials.

3. Schedule a "teaching Mass," during which an adult uses a script that unobtrusively explains the various parts of the liturgy while Mass is in process. Use clear, succinct, bullet-point language that punctuates but does not dominate the experience. Engage children to serve as choir singers, altar servers, procession participants, readers, etc., and arrange for the parents to sit with their child.

4. Schedule events that involve the child as a performer. For example, a play or musical in which heart messages are obvious—as in the programs produced by Creative Ministry Solutions, such as *Follow the Star, We Three Spies, The Case of the Reluctant Innkeeper, Angels Aware.*

5. Role play a desired parent behavior. Take nothing for granted! Prepare parent-child teams to demonstrate vignettes of topics, such as integrating Jesus into conversation, teaching prayer, shaping character, how to correct in love, and how to study a religion homework assignment.

6. Host a family-centered mini-retreat. Structure three or four activities that rotate every half hour. Combine previous suggestions with videos, CDs, DVDs, or episodes of TV shows, cartoons, etc., all where the media message is clear, simple, unmistakable.

7. Celebrate diversity! Organize a way to share family customs or cultural rituals related to birthdays, anniversaries, religious observance of Christmas, Advent, Lent, Easter, and Marian devotions.

8. Schedule a Family Eucharistic-Teaching Evening near Thanksgiving time. Include brief experiences of exposition, adoration, and benediction, and suggest practices for active participation in the Liturgy of the Eucharist. Then encourage families to take a "family watch time" before the Repository of the Blessed Sacrament on Holy Thursday evening and during the parish celebration of Forty Hours.

9. Initiate lifelong support and faith communities at the time of baptism. Network with families who celebrate a baptism within the year. Provide a formative experience to this group of parents once a year. Host an annual anniversary reunion of baptismal families. Offer age-related support in child-rearing. Network with families to organize off-campus discussions in private homes, cafés, or "wherever."

10. Provide easy-on-the-nerves parent formation-education venues that coincide with the child faith-formation sessions. For example:

Small Group Discussion: Invite parents into a classroom to discuss a newsletter, and deliver the literature to the cars of parents who decline the invitation. Provide succinct literature on parenting-support themes. Allow time for reading. Then, in round-robin fashion, ask/answer questions like: 1) How did the newsletter affirm or validate you? 2) How did the newsletter challenge you? 3) Name one action, practice, or behavior that you will apply between now and the next session. Free articles are available at *www.ParentTeacherSupport. org, www.empoweringparents.com*, and many other internet sites as well as in printed material. Prepare parents to serve as discussion facilitators.

- Reading Room: Stock it with parenting literature like *Catholic Update* (Liguori), *Gospel Weeklies* (Pflaum), *Together* (Loyola), etc. Provide coffee, tea, and water.

- Viewing Room: Appoint a space to accommodate DVD or video viewing of presentations like the *Catholicism* series (Bishop Robert Barron) or *Passion and Purpose* and *Seven Pillars of Catholic Spirituality* (Matthew Kelly), or *What Makes Us Catholic?* (Thomas Groome), or *Bible Study* (Ascension Press), as well as other faith-formation programs from various publishers for adults and teens.

- Wifi Space: Publish a list of web-based adult presentations on topics like Sacraments, the Mass, the Bible, Christian Morality, and Catholic Traditions. Include *Busted Halo* web-video series like *Sacraments 101* (Fr. Dave Dwyer, CSP) and *Sacraments 201* (Fr. Steven Bell, CSP), *You Don't Know Jack…about Lent*, Advent, Halloween, Valentine's Day, New Year's, and similar traditions (Fr. Jack Collins, CSP), or church videos and YouTube videos like *Chiseled*, and *Grace*, and *Triduum* (Skit Guys @*www.skitguys.com*).

11. Serve as a clearinghouse for web-based parent resources. Publish links that support faith formation and parenting practices in general.

12. Prior to the opening of the annual faith formation program, schedule an "expect to see you there" registration session. Explain curriculum expectations. Demonstrate a process for home study. Include in the agenda a mini-presentation on what Catholic parenting looks like. (Refer to *www. ParentTeacherSupport.org /Newsletter/Family Faith/ A Guide to Catholic Parenting*.) Videotape or digitize it so that you can offer it on a morning, an afternoon, an evening, before/after the Saturday Vigil Mass, and after Sunday Masses. Post it on the parish website for at-home viewing.

13. Organize parents into assistance groups for faith-formation class sessions. Ask for volunteers in a general setting and/or in a newsletter, but also make personal contact. Typical tasks include setting up a phone chain or group e-mail, writing a class newsletter, serving as a class-starter aide for the first 15 minutes of class (to attend to students, listen to their assignment work, or coach them on prayers and formulas), and assist in arts 'n' crafts projects.

14. Train missionary facilitators. Train a few parents to "break open the word" or other methods of praying with the gospel. Commission them to go out to individual homes to conduct a session with the family so that parents will be more likely to continue the practice on their own. The facilitators might also invite a group of parents into their home for a faith-sharing session. Who knows? Small faith communities might evolve.

15. Suggest Night Prayer Homework. Monthly, send home a night prayer for parents to pray aloud with their children at bedtime. For instance, Psalm 8, Psalm 23, Psalm 139, or a prayer that reads like God is speaking to the child through the parent's voice, or a hymn that conveys God's tender, loving, providential care. The child will absorb God's love and security, and the routine will likely surface favorite phrases or thoughts within the parent that quite possibly will jump-start the parent heart.

Indirect teaching—learning vicariously while attempting to teach children or by accompanying a child to a faith-focused event—is a respectful, easy-on-the-nerves way to evangelize parents. Parents can process information and, in some cases, absorb new information without feeling threatened or needing to reveal inadequacy to their children or to other adults. Ideally, faith-filled information yields to personal, ongoing formation. When formative events touch the heart, they serve as a catalyst for encountering the person of Jesus Christ. Once an adult encounters Jesus, the journey to personal transformation is likely to accelerate.

BACKDOOR EVANGELIZATION AS A STARTING POINT

Backdoor evangelization has its limits and must be accompanied by more full-blown efforts around adult faith formation. Dan Cushing, Director of Adult Faith Formation for the Catholic parishes in Waterloo, Iowa, puts it this way: "There is a place for parents playing games with their children, but it's not a substitute for genuine engagement with adults as adults. Many adults recognize and resent being manipulated in this way" (personal communication, 8/15/15).

Effective adult faith formation builds upon and respects the life experiences of the participants and connects with where adults are in their life journeys. Thus, while teachers and catechists may not be the planners and implementers of adult faith formation ministry, they can open the door for parents who might otherwise not participate. In addition, they can pass along information about faith formation opportunities and encourage parents to take part.

Backdoor evangelization is only meant to nudge parents from the parking lot of stagnation and non-engagement to a fuller involvement with their child, their parish, and their own faith development. Let's move now to other ways to encourage their participation.

FOR REFLECTION AND DISCUSSION

1. Family practices to raise awareness of God's presence are limited only by human creativity, energy level, and time availability. Beyond the examples already mentioned, how do you nourish a sense of spirituality in your life and home?

2. Mary has been named "The Star of the New Evangelization." In what ways is Mary a model and mentor for parents and for children and for family life? How can families put into daily practice the virtues that Mary modeled? What formative Marian experience can your faculty or parish staff offer to parents?

3. What adult faith formation materials, particularly DVDs or website resources, have you found helpful as a support and resource for parents?

Chapter 3

CATECHISTS AS COMPANIONS

The word "companion" comes from the Latin words *com* (together) + *panis* (bread). Translated into our understanding, "companion" means to "share bread together." Breaking bread together is an intimate action. Friends, partners, colleagues, and confidants share meals together. To companion another is to accompany that person, to associate with that person, to complement (to complete him/her), to supplement (make up for what is lacking in him/her). Isn't that exactly what Jesus did for the two disciples who were walking the road to Emmaus (Luke 24:13–32)? They were heavy-hearted about the crucifixion and death of Jesus. They commiserated with each other and shared their confusion, helplessness, and dismay with each other. Jesus joined them on the walk to Emmaus. His appearance was unrecognizable. He met them where they were. He asked them what was on their minds. He responded to their needs. His words restored hope as he interpreted the Scriptures for them. They urged him to stay with them overnight. During the supper meal when he broke the bread, they suddenly realized that their walking companion was Jesus. At that moment he vanished, and they said, "Were not our hearts burning within us while he was talking to us on the road, while he was opening the scriptures to us?"

Catechists are companions when they walk with parents, listening to them, affirming their strengths, supplementing their weaknesses, giving hope, offering support, speaking encouragement, and sharing Scripture. Parents will be receptive to companion catechists who present themselves as colleagues and partners on the journey. They get defensive and resistant when they perceive that the person holding the title of catechist is rigid, judgmental, and critical, or flaunts power, authority, or knowledge.

BEING is the critical factor in the vocation of catechist. The most skilled educational practice in the world (DOING) will fail to evangelize if BEING is neglected. It is the person of the catechist that attracts; not the organization of a class or program tactics. Therefore, before we speak of strategies, techniques, and activities that catechists can use to evangelize, support, and partner with parents, it is essential to reflect a bit on those two critical catechist components: character and function.

THE CHARACTER OF A CATECHIST

Catechists often deal with the same pressures that weigh on parents. Many, after all, are parents themselves. But the life experiences of catechists ignited the fire of evangelization in their souls. Perhaps religious formation was part of their upbringing and drew them to religious study and practices. Or they recognized a religious atmosphere in the home of a friend and desired it for themselves. For some, participation in church/parish life attracted them and they responded by pursuing an adult spiritual life. Ideally, early on they recognized that "passing on the faith" was a *dynamic pursuit*, not a *static objective*. They learned that "the faith" meant getting to know, love, and serve God in imitation of Jesus. They pursued a personal relationship with Jesus. They took advantage of formative experiences like retreats, spiritual direction, prayer groups, and spiritual events.

Humble catechists acknowledge that "there but for the grace of God go I." Translation? Ideally, catechists resist the temptation to judge parents for seeming to be uninvolved in the religious formation of their children. Rather than criticize inactive parents, humble catechists thank God for the grace of their own vocation, and they ask God for the insight, generosity, and creativity needed to fulfill their roles.

All baptized and confirmed Christians possess a God-given duty to evangelize, that is, to introduce every person to Jesus, his message of salvation, and the joy of the gospel. For the catechist, this call includes being a prophetic minister to parents. Both the *United States Catholic Catechism for Adults* (p. 134) and the *General Catechetical Directory* (GDC 237) affirm that lay catechists, more than priests and religious, are in a unique position to directly infuse culture and society with the gospel. Catechists are lay prophets in the church. In her book *The Prophetic Spirit of Catechesis: How We Share the Fire in Our Hearts*, Anne Marie Mongoven, OP, notes that catechists "share in the charism of prophecy, a gift given by God which enables the prophet to nurture, to nourish, and to evoke a consciousness and perception alternative to the consciousness and perception of the dominant culture" (p. 275).

Such compelling language may sound a bit daunting to a catechist. Quite possibly a catechist might want to say, "Hey! I signed on to teach third grade. What do I know about evoking a *perception alternative to the dominant culture?*" Do not be troubled! Pope Francis has explained the vocation of catechist far more simply. He said:

> Catechesis is a vocation: "*being* a catechist," this is the vocation; **not** *working* as a catechist. [Being a catechist embraces your whole life.] It means leading people to encounter Christ by our words and our lives, by giving witness...What attracts is our witness. Being a catechist means witnessing to the faith, being consistent in our personal life....We lead others to Jesus with our words and our lives, with our witness. ... People should see the Gospel, read the Gospel, in our lives. (AUDIENCE TO CATECHISTS, 9/27/13)

We bring Jesus to others by what we are. We evangelize more effectively by our being than by any task we perform. Pope Francis described three elements necessary to BEING a catechist. First comes the *vocation*—a call to be like Jesus. Assigned responsibilities, preparation, and task performance follow—a call to do for/with Jesus.

Pope Francis clarified that the vocation of BEING a catechist calls us to focus on three goals:

1. Being close to Jesus, abiding in him, remaining attached to him like a branch on a vine, listening to him, learning from him, letting ourselves be led by Jesus, remaining in God's presence, in silence, to be looked upon by him;

2. Imitating Jesus by leaving ourselves behind (preconceived notions and ego), going out to encounter others, and being open to others, not rigid;

3. Being courageous…Not being afraid to go with Jesus to the outskirts, going outside our comfort zone, to be faithful, creative, flexible, able to change, able to adapt to the people and situations that are in need of having the gospel proclaimed.

Because catechists share the complexity of contemporary lay life, they are uniquely positioned to be a sign of God's love, to nurture parents, to nourish their weary spirits, and to arouse consciousness of Jesus' personal, passionate love for them. Today, Jesus relies on catechists to be good news and to bring his Good News to children and their parents.

THE FUNCTIONS OF A CATECHIST

A catechist's vocation is a blend of three prioritized functions. The catechist is, first, a witness; then, an educator; and, lastly, a teacher. Let's look at these roles while using Pope Francis, the church's primary catechist, as an example.

1. Witness

"The first form of evangelization is witness" (St. John Paul II, *Redemptoris Missio*, 42). Primarily, a catechist must be an animated witness of the faith. This means that others observe that the catechist has a personal faith relationship with Jesus that sparks life within him/her. The catechist exudes vim, vigor, vitality, and enthusiasm for Jesus, for others, and for the mission of spreading the gospel. Consequently, the energy of the catechist attracts others. It brings light to situations of darkness or confusion.

Pope Francis is the model of an "animated witness." His ready smile and welcoming demeanor make him warm and approachable. In fresh, unrehearsed ways, through word and action, and with a twinkle in his eye, Pope Francis communicates love, and it is infectious! It is the role of the catechist to "go and do likewise" (Luke 10:37).

How can you, the catechist, be an animated witness to parents? In addition to imitating the example of Pope Francis, incorporate the following kinds of practices/attitudes into your interaction with parents:

- Never underestimate the power of a smile. Like the Holy Spirit it "melts the frozen" and "warms the chill" (Sequence of Pentecost).

- Initiate gestures of hospitality and welcome: greeting by name, place cards, including in conversation, asking advice/opinion.

- Display a patient and helpful attitude/approach, especially to parents who are delinquent in responding to your efforts.

- Witness Christian values. Practice redemption and reconciliation—restoring balance to a relationship after an altercation. Demonstrate justice—extending a smile, second chances, an open listening to each parent without partiality or preference.

- Safeguard the human dignity of each parent. Be respectful and confidential.

- Be an agent of hope. "Speak only the good things that people need to hear…things that will help them" (Ephesians 4:29). Or in the words of my mother (and possibly yours), "If you have nothing good to say, say nothing!"

2. Educate

The second function of a catechist is to be an educator, a mentor—one who "walks the walk" through ages and stages. By example and sharing, the catechist illustrates that "the faith" is a dynamic, lively, active process rather than a static condition. The catechist demonstrates that "the faith" is a lifelong, continual conversion to Jesus and a growing relationship with him. Far from appearing to have all the answers, the catechist's life illustrates that growth is a process, that we are all on the journey home. The catechist readies others to encounter Jesus and to be encountered by him. Encounter leads the soul to enter into personal relationship with him.

Each snippet we learn about the life history of Pope Francis educates us. We learn ways that he has grown and changed over time, about mistakes he has made, about admissions of personal sinfulness, about how people have influenced him through the years, and about how events have stretched his soul. We have an indication that he is engaged in a lifelong process of continual conversion of heart, and he does not consider himself "finished." He says such things as "Who am I to judge?" He refers to God and the gospel with an ease and familiarity indicative of an intimate relationship with Jesus. He speaks the language of "we," not "you." He includes himself in the advice or direction that he gives to us. He engages in personal friendship with people whose views are different or who are Catholic but living apart from church discipline. Once again we can hear Jesus whispering: "Go and do likewise."

Catechists are educators when they testify to how grace has been operative throughout the ups and downs of their lives. They educate when they testify to the fidelity of God despite their own imperfections, mistakes, and sins. They understand that faith life is an ongoing process, that faith is more a matter of personal relationship than observance of laws and obligations, and that spiritual maturity is the product of a long season of growing. They embody the *agápē* love that Jesus lived.

How can you, the catechist, be an educator in faith? In addition to imitating the example of Pope Francis, incorporate the following kinds of practices/attitudes into your interaction with parents:

- Prayerfully remember God's presence in your personal history. Trace the ways of grace in your lifeline. Once you "appropriate" your history of grace, you are more likely to share it in unassuming ways. In so doing you will give glory to God and educate parent souls.

- Let your speech convey that you are one with the listener—not above or apart from the person.

- Perform "moral miracles." With God's grace, choose to show love to parents who vex you. Love initiates, welcomes, acknowledges, includes, invites, respects, gives second chances, asks advice, accommodates, and forgives.

- Be a missionary of mercy. See with the heart. As Pope Francis has said, "Live the Gospel, and testify to God's love for all, especially those experiencing difficulties. *Be missionaries of God's love and tenderness!* Be missionaries of God's mercy, which always forgives us, always awaits us and loves us dearly."

- Faith life is a gradual process, a lifelong journey. Share highlights of your faith development history with parents.

- Testify to the difference God makes in your life.

3. Teach

Only if the catechist is first a witness and then an educator can the catechist be an effective teacher (an instructor) of the faith. In culturally age-appropriate ways, the teacher-catechist transmits the word of God from Scripture and Tradition. Additionally, she or he knows well, and integrates content from, the *Catechism of the Catholic Church*. The catechist-teacher realizes that instruction will fall short if he or she is not primarily a witness to Jesus and the joy of his gospel.

Clearly, Pope Francis is a premier teacher. In formal presentations and in informal, impromptu conversations, his message is grounded in Scripture, historical church documents, directives of Vatican Council II, and prescriptions of the *Catechism of the Catholic Church*. He teaches from the heart. He speaks in uncomplicated ways. His messages are clear and succinct and delivered respectfully.

Parents who are minimally, marginally, or insufficiently involved in the faith formation of their children and who are themselves in need of evangelization benefit from catechists, teachers, and administrators who communicate from a mindset of companioning camaraderie rather than a position of power. To be an effective agent of evangelization requires a vocation, a call from God, to be like Jesus in one's own life and daily exchanges. A Jesus-relationship is the essential element of evangelization—not the ability to manage a classroom, design curriculum, or conduct a retreat experience for adults. Actually, it is possible to perform all of those tasks without a prayer life or an energizing relationship with Jesus. But without Jesus at the center of the catechist's heart, those efforts and accomplishments will fail to set hearts aflame! Essential and foundational to the role of catechist is a prayer life centered on Jesus.

Typical practices that nurture intimacy with Jesus include spiritual direction, soul companioning, spiritual disciplines, and praying with the gospel.

- In spiritual direction you share how God has worked in your life since the last direction session, and a trained director listens to the movement of your soul, asks questions that help to clarify your experience, and may suggest a portion of Scripture to pray through. Directors might be clergy, lay persons, or religious. Spiritual Directors International (*www.sdiworld.org*), retreat houses, and spirituality centers are all helpful sources of information about local directors.

- Soul companioning involves two persons who are serious about the spiritual journey, who are willing to share with each other the movement of God in their lives, and who will maintain sacred confidences. They meet for one hour once a month or so. One shares for thirty minutes while the other listens and/or asks clarifying questions. Then the two exchange roles.

- A spiritual discipline is a personal prayer-life plan. For some, it means daily Mass or Eucharistic adoration; for others, praying Liturgy of the Hours or *Lectio Divina* or meditation; for others, fifteen minutes of spiritual reading a day, meditative Rosary, Stations of the Cross, an isolated practice, or a combination of practices. The bottom line is a pattern of prayer that is practiced with consistency. It is a spiritual discipline for catechists to give one hour of preparation time in advance of the week's lesson to plan well and to read and pray through the material in the teacher's guide and its references to the *Catechism* and Scripture.

Cultivate a deep, personal relationship with Jesus. Then, and only then, will witness be possible, followed by the ability to educate (to mentor by example) and then to provide the kind of instruction that feeds the hungers of the human heart. This is what it means to be a companion catechist.

Catechists can companion parents only because they are first and foremost companions of Jesus. Catechists absorb a shepherd-sensitivity because they follow and imitate the Good Shepherd. They identify with Jesus who "saw a large crowd…and had compassion on them, because they were like sheep without a shepherd. So he began teaching them many things" (Mark 6:34). Jesus had compassion…he "suffered with" his people…he moved into action for the sake of his people. Companion catechists are compelled to do likewise.

Jesus calls catechists, teachers, and administrators to companion with compassion—to shepherd after his own heart and to lead with knowledge and understanding (Jeremiah 3:15). With Jesus and through Jesus, catechists develop a shepherd-sensitivity to pasture his sheep, to give them rest, to search out the lost, to bring back the strays, to bind up the injured, and to heal the sick (Ezekiel 34:15–16). These are the ways of compassion.

FOR REFLECTION AND DISCUSSION

1. Pope Francis clarified that the vocation of being a catechist calls us to focus on three goals: being close to Jesus, imitating Jesus, and being courageous. Take time for personal meditation on these points. Though you need to cultivate all three goals, which one is your biggest challenge today?

2. What attracted you to the ministry of faith formation? What attractive characteristics have you observed in other catechists and Catholic school teachers? Brainstorm these questions with faculty/team members. Identify common elements. What commendations surface related to your corporate presence? What recommendations surface related to your corporate presence?

3. Refer to the three goals for nurturing the vocation of catechist (being close to Jesus, imitating Jesus, and being courageous). How can your school or parish assist you to develop each goal?

Chapter 4

SUPPORTING, ENCOURAGING, AND PROVIDING RESOURCES

Prior to his papal election, Cardinal Bergoglio was speaking to Argentina's priests about the need to be pastoral. He said to them: "Jesus teaches us another way: Go out. Go out and share your testimony. Go out and interact with your brothers. Go out and share. Go out and ask. Become the Word in body as well as spirit." This is compassion in action!

The word "compassion" comes from the Latin *com* (together/with) + *passio* (suffer). Translated, "compassion" means "to suffer together, to suffer with" another person. Dictionary definitions illustrate that compassion is action-oriented:

- the act or capacity for sharing the painful feelings of another;

- a feeling of deep sympathy and sorrow for another who is stricken by misfortune, accompanied by a strong desire to alleviate the suffering;

- sympathetic consciousness of others' distress together with a desire to alleviate it;

- tender sorrow for one in misery coupled with an urgent desire to aid or to spare that person from distress;

- a tender concern and power to enter into another's emotional experience;

- to feel motivated to relieve suffering.

Some parents feel disenfranchised, inadequate, over-whelmed, impotent, or any number of things that separate them (or create the perception of separation) from other parents and catechists. And even if they do not feel such conditions, the fact that they are insufficiently involved in the faith formation of their children indicates that they are in need of evangelization. For if experiences of Jesus were common to them, they would automatically bend over backwards to help their children experience Jesus and culti-vate a rich, vibrant relationship with him.

GOING THE EXTRA MILE

An important way to draw parents into fuller engagement with their children's faith formation is through the extension of support, encouragement, and helpful resources. The following two examples illustrate ways to do this.

1. Working around the family schedule

Sister Maria Regis Turney, IHM, worked for three years in a parish in the Archdiocese of Philadelphia. She found a way to reach parents through the sacramental preparation program for children receiving the sacraments of initiation at a later age. Rather than offering a single option, she tailored the program around the varying needs of the parents and families. Older students helped with younger students, so it was possible to reach a wide range of ages within the sessions. An individual family could switch days when necessary to accommodate their schedule. Some parents taught their children at home and gathered once a month to review what they had done and look ahead to the next month's study. "Once a month," she told me,

> families came together for a total-group session and to prepare for a prayer service. As an expression of service, older students helped younger children. For the final prayer service all members of the family came together and then stayed for a concluding lunch. Parents pitched in to help with preparation and clean up. Lunch was uncomplicated. Each family brought what they thought all could eat, and we served it buffet style. Students and their siblings stayed in one group while the parents met

separately. It was a very special time. We became a family, a form of domestic church.

2. Providing at-home resources

Merry Reardon, an experienced catechist and pastoral associate for faith formation, designed an at-home program for sacramental preparation that honors the family as "first place of education in prayer" (*Catechism of the Catholic Church*, 2685) and the parents as primary educators in faith. As a way to provide support and encouragement to parents, she met with them once a month for two years. In the process, parents were given tools to teach their children, as well as tools to share their faith. Parents were provided with a book to use as a vehicle of conversation rather than as a textbook. Merry Reardon told me that

> Parents responded positively to this process. It was a bit scary at first but once they realized that it was meant to be a conversation and that they are not being asked to "know it all," they settled into their roles. Parents were provided with additional digital resources to help support their efforts as well.

CREATIVE APPROACHES

Supporting and encouraging parents requires mercy, tenderness, and heartfelt concern. Be creative in providing information and formation. Build up their knowledge base. Increase their comfort level. Show respect and regard for the challenges they face and the efforts they contribute. By all means, avoid any semblance or perception of callousness, coldheartedness, hard-heartedness, or heartlessness—qualities opposite compassion. Here are some particular ways to do this.

Respecting Time Pressures

Meet parents where they are. Demonstrate that you recognize the restrictions on their time. Honor their needs by streamlining expectations in preclass preparations. Think twice before sending home requests to gather/obtain certain materials for a class project. Employ practices that honor family time needs while supporting the goals of the catechetical program. For instance:

- Plan ahead. Give as much advance notice as possible of upcoming events, preparation needs, and deadlines.

- Post information for parents on the catechetical website so that it is easily accessible. Engage a tech-savvy parent or high-school service-student to maintain the website.

- Consolidate paperwork into a single communication. Condense the information into a single document or include an overview letter with a bulleted item list (with due dates where applicable) for individual attachments.

- Create succinct materials, such as letters, articles, or newsletters, with bulleted items, and avoid dense, crowded print.

- Work with other catechists to coordinate projects so that parents with more than one child in the program are not responsible for multiple tasks within a given week.

- Provide childcare for parent-involved events.

- Make meeting times convenient. Alternate the scheduling of sessions between evening and daytime gatherings, or before or after weekend Masses.

- Make meetings brief and succinct. Stick to the point— the one issue or theme of the occasion. Begin and end on time. Limit sessions to a maximum of ninety minutes. Provide snacks and significant breaks for longer sessions.

- Digitize a meeting to use at a variety of times and post it on your program website.

Demonstrate an "A-plus" attitude

Todd Whitaker's book *Dealing with Difficult Parents* proposes six A+ behaviors as guides for parent-teacher communication: appreciate, affirm, acknowledge, avoid, assume, and admit. Here's how to apply those behaviors to catechist-parent communication.

1. Appreciate the parent for bringing an issue directly to your attention. Verbalize how you welcome his/her input and that you respect him/her for speaking directly to you rather than speaking passively through the gossip mill.

2. Affirm the parent for presenting the issue. Speak in a rational, understanding manner devoid of emotional

tones or the "he said/she said" accusation-style of communication.

3. Acknowledge the parent's feelings. Don't downplay or argue with parents over the perception, but try to listen to what needs underlie their emotions.

4. Avoid becoming defensive. The moment you feel the urge to justify an action or your position, to protect yourself, or to guard or to secure your program, the ego emerges. Once ego takes over, the issue is no longer about the student or parent; it becomes about you!

5. Assume positive intentions and motivations on the part of the parent. Give the benefit of the doubt to parent behavior or lack of involvement. Trust that parents intend the best for their children and that if an event does not turn out well it is due to insufficient knowledge or weak human nature and not a lack of desire.

6. Admit wrongdoing or guilt. Be secure enough to apologize. Or, even if you are not at fault, be humble enough to say something like, "I regret that this issue has been so stressful." Or, "I can explain why I made that decision but it does not excuse the hurt that resulted."

PARTNER WITH PARENTS

Communicate. Show respect, consideration, and concern. Encourage. Be positive and dependable, open and receptive to parent suggestion/input. Be collaborative, helpful, sharing, and caring. Be supportive; give constructive advice; and, rather than being a judge, practice the role of a companion, one who walks the same road. Let your interactions reflect four "WITH" qualities: W (wisdom), I (initiative), T (truth), and H (hope).

Wisdom

"Wisdom from above is first pure, then peaceable, gentle, willing to yield, full of mercy and good fruits, without a trace of partiality or hypocrisy" (James 3:17). Wisdom is the image of God's goodness (Wisdom 7:26). How well does wisdom characterize your interaction with parents? Here are three ways to hone the skills of wisdom.

I. ADOPT A PROACTIVE PERSPECTIVE

Recognize that parents are doing what they believe to be the best for their child. If the results are inadequate, a compassionate response rests with the catechist, teacher, or administrator to provide helpful formation, information, and support. Anticipate what might go wrong, and make contingency plans or adaptations. Address sensitive issues in private. Provide parents with skill training—both formation and information. Prayerfully script remarks in advance of a meeting. For example, "I value the perspective that you shared. I will need time to reflect on it." Or, "This is new information to me. I will pray over it."

2. DISPLAY PROFESSIONAL MANNERS

Filter out personal ego issues and establish personal boundaries. Use a respectful tone of voice and body language. Be kind but firm. Convey a sense of quiet confidence. Replace a confrontational, argumentative, or defensive attitude with a helpful, problem-solving approach.

3. STRIVE TO RESPOND RATHER THAN REACT

Focus on your own behavior. If a parent expresses anger or accusations, do not respond in like-kind. Take the "high road." Never raise your voice, use sarcasm, argue, or treat a parent rudely. Avoid power struggles. Do not let angry or self-righteous emotions dictate your behavior. You may not be able to control your feelings, but it is essential that you control your actions. Think "imaginary audience!" When you speak with a parent imagine that others can observe you and hear you. Conduct yourself accordingly.

Initiative

"Proclaim the message; be persistent whether the time is favorable or unfavorable, convince, rebuke, and encourage with the utmost patience in teaching..." (2 Timothy 4:2–5). Initiate conversations with parents. Be persistent! Provide an experience of consistency, continuity, and predictability. Encourage parents by being a mirror or model of behaviors that are effective in evangelizing their children. Affirm and validate parent input whenever possible. Be a catechist who is willing to go the extra mile! Strive to create a rapport with the parent community and to exercise proactive leadership to maintain the rapport. Here are two ideas for doing this.

I. CREATE A RAPPORT

Face-to-face contact, phone calls, electronic newsletters, or printed memos build a rapport before the school year begins and feed it throughout the year. When you need to communicate a common message to several parents, write a script to use. After a parent expresses a concern or criticism, follow up as soon as possible. Be personable, make eye contact, and smile. Elicit parent opinions and invite them to share expertise. Acknowledge publicly parent efforts and contributions.

2. EXERCISE PROACTIVE LEADERSHIP

Be accessible, visible, and approachable. Avoid the perception of having "favorites" or of seeking input or respecting the opinions of a limited group of parents. Demonstrate a spirit of equanimity, that is, mental calmness, composure, and evenness of temper, especially in a difficult situation. Give responsibility to parents. Link active parents with less active ones to fulfill a task. Organize open, optional planning meetings or advisory meetings. Build leadership teams.

Truth

Say only the good things that people need to hear, things that will really help them. *"Speak the truth in love"* (Ephesians 4:15). Truth is foundational to self-respect and to relationship. If I cannot trust you, or you cannot trust me, we cannot grow in relationship. Respect and personal integrity go hand-in-hand. Both are rooted in truth. And truth is rooted in God.

If the truth that you need to speak is sensitive or hard to hear, let your purpose for speaking be to build up and support the parent. Communicate an attitude that says, "If the situation were reversed I would want you to tell me." In its origin, speaking the truth in love has to do with what we believe and teach about Jesus. It is an extension of gospel principles, mutual respect, and honoring persons. The kind of loyalty, consideration, and compassion that is due a member of your own family is due to all people. Speak the way that you want others to speak to your loved ones. Be kind, gentle, and respectful in tone, facial expression, and body language. Be constructive. Work to resolve a problem rather than exacerbate or inflame it. Nurture the relationship.

Make truth the foundation of your interactions with parents. Speak from a place of principle, not power. Communicate in face-saving ways that lead to conversion and connection. Here are ten hallmarks for being an agent of truth.

1. PREPARE FOR A PARENT CONVERSATIONS BY APPLYING THE THINK TEST.

T – Is it **True**? Whose truth is it? Is it a matter of principle or personal preference/ego?

H – Is it **Helpful**? Are chances better than not that the parent will be able to "hear" what you say and be able to apply your information?

I – Is it **Important**? Is the topic vital to the process of "stimulating one another to love and good deeds" (Hebrews 10:24)?

N – Is it **Necessary**? Will silence on this issue cause more harm than good?

K – Is it **Kind**? Is the information you intend to present good-hearted, thoughtful, gracious, courteous, and charitable? And will it be spoken with tenderness and sensitivity?

If a person feels unloved or disrespected, your words will fall on deaf ears. If this is a parent's perception, it is best to remain silent and let another catechist, teacher, or administrator speak what needs to be communicated.

2. PRAY BEFORE A PARENT CONVERSATION. Ask the Holy Spirit to remove any bias, preconceived notions, or personal hurts/annoyances/grievances. Then seek to be filled with the breath of God, the mindset of Jesus. Breathe deeply several times while praying this request. Ask Jesus to go into the meeting space before you and to sit in the conversation circle. Place an extra chair at the table or space. Let it serve as a reminder that Jesus is present.

3. SPEAK FROM OBSERVATION, NOT FROM HEARSAY OR PERSONAL FEELINGS. It causes more harm than good to say, "I cannot tell you who said this but ..." or "I heard that you..." Such remarks shift the focus from the issue that needs discussion to wanting to discover the source of the information.

4. SPEAK WITH RESPECT, REVERENCE, AND ENCOURAGEMENT. Remember that "hearts have been broken by harsh words spoken that sorrow can never set right" (Margaret Elizabeth Sangster).

5. AVOID INFLAMMATORY VOCABULARY AND AN ACCUSATORY OR JUDGMENTAL TONE. Speak with a sense of loving detachment rather than emotional investment. Eliminate from your words, tone, or body language any trace of taking personal pleasure at correcting, smugness, or self-righteousness.

6. SPEAK KINDLY BUT FIRMLY. "Let no evil talk come out of your mouths, but only what is useful for building up, as there is need, so that your words may give grace to those who hear" (Ephesians 4:29).

7. SPEAK BRIEFLY. BE CLEAR. Speak to the point. Resist the temptation to defend your position or to repeat yourself.

8. THINK BEFORE YOU SPEAK. Respond rather than react to a parent prompt. Have "ready expressions" to say, such as: "Let me pray about it, and then we'll discuss it more thoroughly" or "I need to think this through before I respond to you."

9. ENCOURAGE PARENTS WITH "EFFECTIVE PRAISE"—FEED-BACK THAT IS AUTHENTIC, SPECIFIC, IMMEDIATE, AND PRIVATE. Say what you mean and mean what you say; have no ulterior motives or passive-aggressive messages.

10. STRIVE TO BE WHO YOU SAY YOU ARE. When you fail, acknowledge it, apologize, and very simply explain your plan for amendment.

Hope

"[We know that] suffering produces endurance, and endurance produces character [virtue], and character produces hope, and hope does not disappoint us, because God's love has been poured into our hearts through the Holy Spirit that has been given to us" (Romans 5:3–5).

Parents need catechists, teachers, and administrators to be agents of hope, human vessels who bring clarity and direction to parent aspirations, goals, and desires for their children. Here are three efforts to further that goal.

1. ADOPT THE ATTITUDE OF "IMPROVEMENT VS. PERFECTION"

Any positive growth is movement in the right direction. Be patient with small steps and the distinct possibility that we may never see the end result. Don't take yourself too seriously. Trust that God will work through your good will, even if you do not recognize it. Sow the seed, and let the reaping be in God's good time.

2. FACILITATE AN "H-CULTURE": HOPE, HUMOR, HELPFULNESS, AND HOLINESS

Draw upon examples of people who overcame obstacles of disability or life circumstances. Pass along that information to parents whose children struggle with learning challenges. Weave messages of hope into conversation and newsletters. Foster the dignity of parents by emphasizing how they and their children are created in the image of God (*Imago Dei*).

3. PROVIDE FORMATIVE SUPPORT

In addition to learning how to nurture faith in their children, parents desire support for fostering self-esteem, self-discipline, resiliency, character development, etc. They want information that is succinct, such as articles, newsletters, bulletins, or quick-to-read messages sent electronically. Resources are available from various sources. Distribute information through handouts, discussion groups, in-services, or presentations.

The grace of God calls catechists, teachers, and administrators to meet parents where they are. Companion them as fellow pilgrims on the journey home. Convey sensitivity to their needs. Respect the time pressures that strain and constrain parents. Respect your own need for balance. Demonstrate an A+ attitude with parents. Extend to them courtesy and a cooperative spirit. Assume the role of partner. Hone the "with" skills: wisdom, initiative, truth, and hope. This is what it means to companion with compassion.

FOR REFLECTION AND DISCUSSION

"Wisdom from above is first pure, then peaceable, gentle, willing to yield, full of mercy and good fruits, without a trace of partiality or hypocrisy" (James 3:17). How well does wisdom characterize your interaction with parents?

Compassion implies action! What actions of yours demonstrate compassion for parents in the catechetical or school community?

Consider the term "EGO" to mean "Edge God Out." Recall an instance when your ego dominated a parent conference. If you had a "do over," how would you conduct the conversation?

Going to the "outskirts"—to the marginalized—implies going the extra mile! In what ways can your faculty/ministerial team take on the goal of evangelizing parents?

Chapter 5

FROM PARKING LOT TO PARTICIPATION

"What is equal to training the soul and forming the mind of one that is young?" Nothing known to me! The need for soul formation is as prominent today as it was when St. John Chrysostom asked that question of fourth-century parents. The home—then and now—serves as the first and foremost place for soul formation. Parent influence has such exponential value that it is extremely difficult to compensate for disengaged parents. Vatican Council II understood this sacred dynamic and hailed parents as "the primary and principal educators."

Without a doubt the primary place for catechesis is the home. Parents are the "first heralds" of the gospel to their children (*Familiaris Consortio, 39*). Forming the soul of a child is a challenging mission for any parent because human capacity is limited. Nurturing a strong partnership with parents is a necessity in leading children to a God-relationship.

Parents who meet the call to form their children in faith are tutored by the very teachings they share with their children. The same is true of catechists. Parents who review assignments with their children hone their own faith skills in the process. St. John Paul II expressed the dynamic this way: "Parents themselves profit from the effort that this demands of them, for in a catechetical dialogue of this sort each individual both receives and gives" (*Catechesi Tradendae*, 68).

Faith instruction of children by parents is more effective than instruction by any other catechist. This is why St. John Paul II proclaimed:

> Christian parents must strive to follow and repeat, within the setting of family life, the more methodical teaching received elsewhere. The fact that these truths about the main questions of faith and Christian living are thus repeated within a family setting impregnated with love and respect will often make it possible to influence the children in a decisive way for life...Family catechesis therefore precedes, accompanies and enriches all other forms of catechesis. (Catechesi Tradendae, 68)

When parents are infused with a loving God-relationship, they grow the confidence to share the faith. This makes partnership with parents a critical part of our catechetical efforts. "The Christian community must give very special attention to parents. By means of personal contact, meetings, courses and also adult catechesis directed toward parents, the Christian community must help them assume their responsibility—which is particularly delicate today—of educating their children in the faith" (GDC 227).

Hear in the words of Isaiah 50:4 the focus for ministry to parents: "The Lord God has given me a well-trained tongue, that I might know how to speak to the weary a word that will rouse them." Many parents are weary. They live incredibly complex lives, frequently isolated and disconnected from a support system, feeling drained and "running on empty." Some feel overwhelmed by life's demands, scattered, or disorganized. Often there exists a gap in their personal faith formation—a spiritual vacuum—since their formative education was limited to preadolescence or adolescence. For varied reasons, many parents think that they are inadequate to provide faith formation for their children. Proactively consider how best to approach parents, how to advertise programs, and how to orchestrate events. Be intent on soothing, comforting, clarifying, and enlightening parents. Be an agent of calm in their all-too-harried lives. Avoid or eliminate any gesture or activity that has the potential to alienate, anger, annoy, irritate, insult, agitate, distress, or upset.

To move parents from the parking lot to participation, enable parents to function for their children as the "I" in the word "evangelize:" to *initiate* age-appropriate spiritual formation, to *invite* their children to prayerful encounters with Jesus, to *infuse* the home with an awareness of the sacred, and to *inspire* their family by their personal example. Develop quick-paced, brief information sessions on these topics. Digitize presentations. Post them on the parish website. And/or provide succinct newsletters. Get creative! Imagine performing a topical infomercial five minutes before the Sunday liturgy! Engage families to perform vignettes that illustrate the issue.

Speak to parent hearts before speaking to their heads. When formative events touch the heart, they serve as a catalyst for encountering the person of Jesus Christ. Use Scripture and sacred music to create an ambiance for parents to hear Jesus speak to their hearts. Orchestrate a holy hour for parents. Use candlelight, soft music, a script for guided adoration, and prayers or readings that massage the heart.

Energize, empower, and engage parents as colleagues and partners. Adapt an interactive, social, conversational approach. Provide easy-on-the-nerves, teachable moments. During indirect learning events, the Spirit tutors parent hearts while they focus on an activity with their children.

Simplify the message! Highlight that passing on the faith is a dynamic pursuit—not a static objective, not a collection of "Dos and Don'ts." "Faith" means getting to know, love, and serve God in imitation of Jesus. Assure parents that faith-relationship grows with age and experience.

Go the extra mile! Involve parents more directly in the program and parish.

- Connect young families with seasoned families.

- At a social, ask parishioners to host a table and to personally invite two new families as guests.

- Establish a "Plus One" policy in which the usual family participants each bring one additional family to Mass, to a social, to Forty Hours, to seasonal prayer services, etc.

- Elicit seasoned families to serve as host families to families who are new to the program or parish. A host family provides orientation to the school or faith formation program, explains the services available in the parish, and makes the new family aware of parish ministries. The hosts invite the new family to join them at Mass for special occasions like Thanksgiving, Advent by Candlelight, Palm Sunday, or the May Procession. They invite them to work together at a parish function and to socialize with a few other families at the host home.

- Partition the parish or program into units of fifteen families. Elicit volunteers to serve as partition captains. Make it their responsibility to contact the families throughout the year to extend invitations to events, to request participation in a particular project, and to encourage registration at the parish men's and/or women's retreat or parish clubs.

- Encourage catechists to assume a missionary role—to visit the family of each student, to demonstrate a technique for praying with the Sunday gospel, and to urge parents to imitate the prayer exercise weekly.

It is my hope that this book will provide catechists with a treasure chest of possibilities for moving parents from the parking lot to fuller participation in the faith formation of their children. May the ideas presented stir your own creative juices to generate additional ideas. And may collaboration with other catechists and other parishes cultivate within you the audacious attitude called forth by Pope Francis. When addressing catechists (9/27/13) he said:

> Let us remain with Christ—abiding in Christ—and let us always try to be one with him. Let us follow him, let us imitate him in his movement of love, in his going forth to meet humanity. Let us go forth and open doors. Let us have the audacity to mark out new paths for proclaiming the Gospel.

Open doors, ring telephones, and think outside the box to help parents to mark out new paths. Sow the seeds of systematic change however you can, all the while putting your energy, effort, and enthusiasm at the service of what you *can* do rather than being paralyzed by what you *cannot* do. In solidarity with St. Paul, I say: "I am convinced and sure of this very thing, that he who began a good work in you will carry it on to completion until the day of Christ Jesus" (Philippians 1:6). Modern wisdom says: "God's love does not call where God's grace cannot keep." You have what you need to respond in fruitful ways.

Both catechists and parents are charged to lead children to a personal relationship with Jesus Christ and to form children in the faith of the Catholic Church. Either or both of you may sometimes feel inadequate and unqualified for the task. When those moments of doubt attack, take comfort in the truth that "God does not call the qualified. God qualifies the called." Parents are the primary formators of faith who can bring their children to Jesus. And you, dear catechist, are the catalyst who can move parents from the parking lot to participation.